G-5278

THE BOOK OF

CALL &

RESPONSE

You Sing, I Sing

REVISED EDITION

Compiled by John M. Feierabend

GIA PUBLICATIONS, INC. · CHICAGO

Also by John M. Feierabend, published by GIA Publications, Inc.:
The Book of Echo Songs
The Book of Fingerplays and Action Songs
The Book of Children's SongTales
The Book of Beginning Circle Games
The Book of Songs and Rhymes with Beat Motions
The Book of Pitch Exploration
The Book of Movement Exploration (*with Jane Kahan*)

For infants and toddlers:
The Book of Lullabies
The Book of Wiggles and Tickles
The Book of Simple Songs and Circles
The Book of Bounces
The Book of Tapping and Clapping

On compact disc for infants and toddlers:
'Round and 'Round the Garden: Music in My First Year!
Ride Away on Your Horses: Music, Now I'm One!
Frog in the Meadow: Music, Now I'm Two!

On DVD and Compact Disc by Peggy Lyman and John M. Feierabend:
Move It! Expressive Movements with Classical Music
Move It 2! Expressive Movements with Classical Music

G-5278
The Book of Call and Response (Revised Edition)
Compiled by John M. Feierabend
www.giamusic.com/feierabend

"Hashewie" (pp. 54–55) comes from the collection *Roots and Branches* by Patricia Shehan Campbell, Ellen McCullough-Brabson, and Judith Cook Tucker, © 1994, assigned 2009 to Plank Road Publishing, Inc. Used with permission.

Copyright © 2020, 2003
GIA Publications, Inc.
7404 S. Mason Avenue
Chicago, IL 60638

Table of
Contents

Introduction

Whether used around a campfire, in the classroom, or on a family road trip, everyone can enjoy Call and Response songs from the start. Unlike most songs, which take time to master, the songs in this book enable everyone to sing immediately. The leader sings a phrase and the group sings back a pre-learned reply.

Call and Response songs are like echo songs because the leader and the group take turns singing. They differ from echo songs because the groups' sung response differs from the leader's part, requiring the group to pre-learn and remember what they will sing.

If echo songs are like soliloquies, then Call and Response songs are musical dialogues, allowing for greater richness and complexity.

Songs such as these have thrived in work settings such as in the fields or on ships. They helped pass the time and keep the workers in sync with each other. All of the Call and Response songs in this book have been passed down from generation to generation.

Everyone loves Call and Response songs because they are so accessible and lively.

Enjoy!

John M. Feierabend

Snaps & Snails

Songs about boys

John Belly Grow

Green Green Rocky

Leader: Green, green   Group: Rock - y,

Prom - e - nade   in   green,   Rock - y,

Tell   me   who   you   love,   Rock - y,

Tell   me   in - side   out,   Rock - y,

Tell   me   up - side - down,   Rock - y.

All   a - round   the   block,   Rock - y,

All   a - round   the   town,   Rock - y.

Boney Was a Warrior

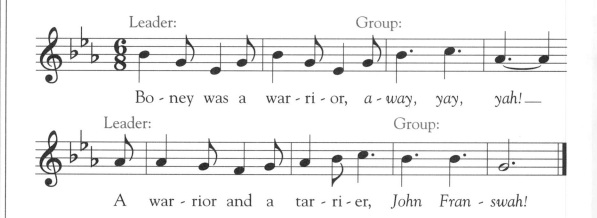

Leader: Bo - ney was a war - ri - or, *a - way, yay, yah!* —

Group:

Leader: A war - rior and a tar - ri - er, *John Fran - swah!*

Group:

Additional Verses

2. Boney fought the Prooshians...
   Boney fought the Prooshians...
3. Moscow was a-blazin'...
   Boney was a-ragin'....
4. Boney went to Elba...
   Boney he came back again...
5. Boney went to Waterloo...
   There he got his overthrow...
6. Boney broke his heart and died...
   Away in Saint Helena...
7. Drive her, Captain, drive her...
   Drive her, Captain, drive her...
8. Give he top gallant sails...
   'Tis a weary way to Baltimore...

"Boney" is Napolean Bonaparte.

Santa Anna

Leader:
O San - ta An - na gained the day,

Group:
Hoo - ray, San - ty An - na!

Leader:
He lost it— once but— gained it twice,

Group:
All— on the plains of Mex - i - co.

Additional Verses

2. And General Taylor ran away...
   He ran away to Monterey...
3. Oh, Santa Anna fought for fame...
   And there's where Santa gained his name...
4. Oh, Santa Anna fought for gold...
   And the deeds he done have oft been told...

5. And Santa Anna fought for his life...
   But he gained his way in the terrible strife...
6. Oh, Santa Anna's day is o'er...
   And Santa Anna will fight no more...
7. I thought I heard the Old Man say...
   He'd give us grog this very day...

Little Johnny Brown

All:
Lit - tle John - ny Brown, lay your com - fort down,

Lit - tle John - ny Brown, lay your com - fort down.

Leader: Group:
Fold down your cor - ner, John - ny Brown,

Fold down your cor - ner, John - ny Brown.

Fold down your cor - ner, John - ny Brown,

Fold down your cor - ner, John - ny Brown.

Motions

Children stand in a circle clapping hands on the off beats. During the first two phrases one child walks around the inside of the circle carrying a handkerchief. During the call and response the child in the center sets the kerchief down in front of a selected child and sings the leader part asking him/her to fold the corners into the center of the kerchief (one corner for each phrase). At the end of the song the selected child picks up the kerchief and the game repeats from the beginning.

Sugar & Spice

Songs about girls

C-Line Woman

Leader: Group:

C - Line wom - an, C - Line,

She drinks cof - fee, C - Line,

She drinks tea, C - Line,

In the can - dle light, C - Line.

The Churchyard Door

Leader:

A wo - man stood at the church - yard door,

Group:

woo - oo - oo - oo, woo - oo - oo - oo.

Additional Verses

2. And she had not been there before...
3. Oh, six long corpses were carried in...
4. So very long and very thin...
5. The woman to the corpses said...
6. "Will I be thus when I am dead?"...
7. The corpses to the woman said
   (*scream* "Ahhhhh")

Darling Rosie

Leader: Ro - sie, dar - ling Ro - sie. Group: Ha, ha, Ro - sie.

Ro - sie, dar - ling Ro - sie, Ha, ha, Ro - sie.

Way down south in Bal - ti - more, Ha, ha, Ro - sie,

Need no car - pet on the floor, Ha, ha, Ro - sie.

Verse 2

Grab your partner and follow me...
Let's go down by Gallee...
Rosie darling hurry...
If you don't mind you're gonna get left...

Verse 3

You steal my partner, you won't steal
    no more...
Better stay away from my back door...
Stop right still and study yourself...
See that fool where she got left...

Motions

The group forms two circles, one inside the other. Those two circles walk around in the same direction. During the first verse one child walks "through the alley" between the two circles in the opposite direction. During the second verse the single child selects one child from either circle and the two of them walk "through the alley." During the third verse the original child goes to the vacant space and the game is started over with the chosen child walking "through the alley."

Sally Brown

Call:
Oh, Sal - ly Brown, she's the gal for me, boys!

Response:
Roll, boys, roll, boys, roll!

Call:
Sal - ly Brown, she's the gal for me, boys!

Response:
Way high, Miss Sal - ly Brown!

Verse 2

We're away down south, down
  south, boys!
Roll, boys, roll, boys, roll!
Bound away down south, down
  south, boys!
Way high, Miss Sally Brown!

Verse 3

There's forty fathoms or more below,
  boys!
Roll, boys, roll, boys, roll!
Forty fathoms or more below, boys!
Way high, Miss Sally Brown.

Jane, Jane

Additional Verses:

2. Hey, hey…
   My Lordy, Lord…
   I'm a gonna buy…
   Three hunting dogs…
   One for to run…
   One for to shout…
   One to talk to…
   When I go out…

3. Hey, hey…
   My Lordy, Lord…
   I'm a gonna buy…
   Three muley cows*…
   One a-for to milk…
   One to plow my corn…
   One for to pray…
   One Christmas Morn'…

4. Hey, hey…
   My Lordy, Lord…
   I'm a gonna buy…
   Three little bluebirds…
   One a-for to weep…
   One for to mourn…
   One for to grieve…
   When I am gone…

5. Hey, hey…
   My Lordy, Lord…
   I'm a gonna buy…
   Three mockingbirds…
   One a-for to whistle…
   One a-for to sing…
   One a-for to do…
   Most any little thing…

*"Muley cows" are cows without horns.

Miss Julie Ann Johnson

Verse 2

Oh, where's my Julie... (x2)
She's gone to Dallas... (x2)

Verse 3

Going to catch the train... (x2)
Going to find Julie... (x2)

Verse 4

Going to hug my Julie... (x2)
Miss Julie Ann Johnson... (x2)

Miss Mary Mack

Leader:　　　　　　　　　　　Group:

Miss Mar - y Mack,　　　Mack,　　　Mack.

Additional Verses

All dressed in black, black, black.
With silver buttons, buttons, buttons.
All down her back, back, back.
She asked her mother, mother, mother.
For fifty cents, cents, cents.
To see the elephant, elephant, elephant.
Jump over the fence, fence, fence.
He jumped so high, high, high.
He reached the sky, sky, sky.
And he didn't come back, back, back.
'Til the fourth of July, ly, ly.

Hand Clapping Pattern

Cross (Arms crossed on chest.)
Down (Tap both hands on own legs.)
Clap (Clap own hands.)
Right (Clap right hand to partner's right hand.)
Clap (Clap own hands.)
Left (Clap left hand to partner's left hand.)
Clap (Clap own hands.)
Both (Clap both hands to both hands of your partner.)

Little Speck O' Lady

Motions

All hold hands in a circle with one girl in the center (only girls stand in the center). The circle walks in one direction; the girl in the center walks in the opposite direction. At "O Miss Sally Mae" the circle stops and taps the beat on their legs while the girl selects another girl to swing by the right arm. At the end of the song, the new girl stays in the center, and the first one returns to the circle.

There Was an Old Woman...

Leader:

There was an old wom-an all skin and bones.

Group:

Oo - oo - oo - oo.

Additional Verses

2. She lived down by the old church yard...

3. One night she thought she'd take a walk...

4. She walked down by the old grave yard...

5. She saw some bones a-laying around...

6. She went to the closet to get a broom...

7. She opened the door and "BOO!" (Shout)

Won't You Go My Way?

Leader: I met her in the morn-ing, Group: Won't you go my way?

I met her in the morn-ing, Won't you go my way?

Additional Verses

2. In the morning bright and early...
3. Oh, Julia, Anna, Maria...
4. I asked that girl to marry...
5. She said she'd rather tarry...
6. Oh, marry, never tarry...

On the Phone

Someone's on the Phone

Person 1:

Ring! Hel-lo. Hey there Su-san, some-one's on the phone.

Person 2:

Well, if it's my friend Jen-ny tell her I'm at home.

All:

We're sing-in' tick-a, tack-a, tick-a, tack-a, wal-ly woo-woo,

tick-a, tack-a, tick-a, tack-a, wal-ly woo-woo.

With each repeat, the "Second person"
assumes the "First person's" part.

The Telephone

Hey, Mar - gy, I think I hear my name.

Hey, Mar - gy, I think I hear it a - gain.

You're want - ed on the tel - e - phone.

If it is - n't Char - lie I'm not at home.

With a ring - ding, ding - a - ding ding, Oh, yeah.

With a ring - ding, ding - a - ding ding.

*Person 2 now assumes the role of Person 1
and names a new person.*

Fur, Feathers & Fins

Blackhorn

Hunter: ... Group:

Black-horn! Black-horn! But-ter and milk and bar-ley corn.

Hunter:

How man-y geese have you to-day?

Group:

More than you can catch and car-ry a-way.

Motions

All children are at one end of the room. One person (the hunter) is in the middle of the room and sings. The Call and Response is sung. At the end of the song all children run to the other end of the room. The hunter tries to tag as many children as possible. Those who are tagged stay in the center and help tag the others on the repeat. Continue the game until all have been tagged. The last person tagged becomes the new hunter.

Carrion Crow

A car-rion crow sat on an oak,

Der-ry, der-ry, der-ry dek-ko;

A car-rion crow sat on an oak, Watch-ing a tai-lor

mend his cloak, Sing heigh-o, the car-ri-on crow,

Der-ry, der-ry, der-ry dek-ko!

Verse 2

O wife, bring me my old bent bow,
  Derry, derry, derry, dekko.
O wife, bring me my old bent bow
That I may shoot yon carrion crow;
Sing heigh-o, the carrion crow,
  Derry, derry, derry, dekko.

Verse 3

The tailor shot and missed his mark,
  Derry, derry, derry, dekko.
The tailor shot and missed his mark
And shot his old sow through the
  heart,

Sing heigh-o, the carrion crow,
  Derry, derry, derry, dekko.

Verse 4

The sow died and the bells did toll,
  Derry, derry, derry, dekko.
The sow died and the bells did toll
And the little pigs prayed for the old
  sow's soul,
Sing heigh-o, the carrion crow,
  Derry, derry, derry, dekko.

Chinene Nye? (What Is Big?) *Angola*

Leader: Chi - ne - ne nye? Group: Chi - ne - ne o - nja - mba.

Chi - ne - ne nye? Chi - ne - ne o - nja - mba. Ki - nya - ma vi -

o - si Ka ku li u - kua - vo.

Leader: "Elenalo"
Group: "Hale"

Leader: Yen - de, yen - de Group: Ha - le!

Yen - de, yen - de Ha - le!

E - le - na - lo lo - ma - la va - he! Ha - le!

Ma - la - nga lo - ma - la va - he! Ha - le!

Nge - ve lo - ma - la va - he! Ha - le!

Ho - si lo - ma - la va - he! Ha - le!

Ngue lo - ma - la va - he! Ha - le!

E - le - na - lo lo - ma - la va - he! Ha - le!

As this is a work song, repeat until the work is done.

Ending:
Leader: "O wi" (Work is done)
Group: "O co!" (Yes indeed!)

After the repeat of the first three lines the leader changes the song by saying "Elenalo" (Chameleon) which means he can change his song just as a chameleon changes colors. The group responds by saying "Hale" (Crab) which means they can follow the leader just as a crab can go in any direction. Allow time for the dialogue.

General Translation

What is big? An elephant is big.
He is the largest animal in the world.
Go crab.
Chameleon and his children!
Cheetah and his children!
Hippopotamus and his children!
Lion and his children!
Leopard and his children!
Chameleon and his children!

Did You Feed My Chickens?

Leader: Lit - tle girl, lit - tle girl! **Group:** Yes, sir.

Did you feed my chick-ens? Yes, sir.

What did you feed them? Corn and wheat.

What did you feed them? Corn and wheat.

Verse 2

Little girl, little girl! *Yes sir.*
Did you feed my cat? *Yes, sir.*
What did you feed it?
  Bread and milk.(x2)

Verse 3

Little boy, little boy! *Yes, sir.*
Did you feed my horse? *Yes, sir.*
What did you feed it?
  Corn and hay. (x2)

Verse 4

Little boy, little boy! *Yes, sir.*
Did you feed my sheep? *Yes, sir.*
What did you feed them?
  Oats and barley. (x2)

Did You Feed My Cow?

Additional Verses & Motions

Verse 2

Did you milk her good? *Yes, ma'am.*
Did you milk her like you should?
  Yes, ma'am.
How did you milk her? *Squish, squish,
  squish.*
  (Imitate milking motions with hands.)
How did you milk her? *Squish, squish,
  squish.*

Verse 3

Did my cow get sick? *Yes ma'am.*
Was she covered with tick? *Yes ma'am.*
How did she die? *Mm Mm Mm.*
  (Shake head back and forth.)
How did she die? *Mm Mm Mm.*

Verse 4

Did the buzzards come? *Yes ma'am.*
Did the buzzards come? *Yes ma'am.*
How did they come? *Flap, flap, flap.*
  *(With hands under arms, imitate wings
  flapping.)*
How did they come? *Flap, flap, flap.*

Grizzly Bear

Call: Response:

Tell me who is a griz-ze-ly, a griz-ze-ly bear?—

Tell me who is a griz-ze-ly, a griz-ze-ly bear?—

He had the great long tush-es *like a griz-ze-ly bear,*—

He had the great long tush-es *like a griz-ze-ly bear,*—

He made a noise in the bot-tom *like a griz-ze-ly bear,*—

He made a noise in the bot-tom *like a griz-ze-ly bear.*—

Hill and Gully Rider

Leader:
Group:

Hill and gul - ly rid - er, *hill and gul - ly.*

Fine

Hill and gul - ly rid - er, *hill and gul - ly.*

Took my horse and come down, *hill and gul - ly,*

But my horse done stum - ble down, *hill and gul - ly,*

D.C. al Fine

And the night time come a - tumb - lin' down, *hill and gul - ly.*

Mule Song

Leader: Whoa, mule! Group: Can't get the sad - dle on.

Whoa, mule! Can't get the sad - dle on.

Verse 2

Catch the mule!...

Verse 3

Ride the mule!...

Verse 4

Run, mule!...

John the Rabbit (Version 1)

Leader: Oh, John, the rab - bit, Oh yes; Group: Oh, John, the rab - bit, Oh yes;

Had a might - y fine hab - it, Oh yes;

Of jump - ing in my gar - den; Oh yes.

And eat - ing up my spin - ach, Oh yes;

He ate po - ta - toes, Oh yes; And sweet to - ma - toes, Oh yes;

And if I live, Oh yes; To see next fall, Oh yes;

I won't plant, Oh yes; A gar - den at all, Oh yes.

John the Rabbit (Version 2)

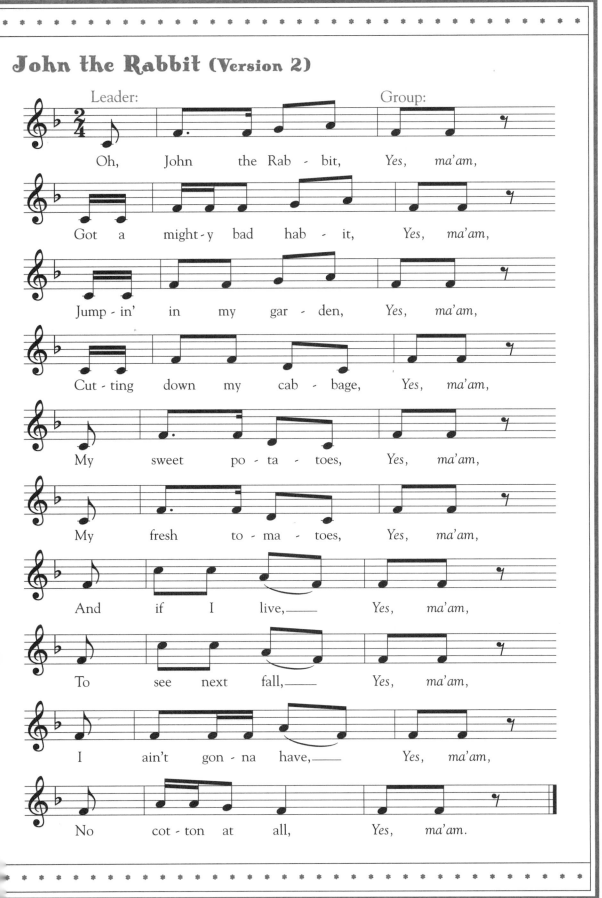

Lucy Rabbit

Leader:

Group:

Lu - cy Rab - bit, Hey, Hey!

In my gar - den, Hey, Hey!

Cut my col - lards, Hey, Hey!

Cut my car - rots, Hey, Hey!

Cut my tur - nips, Hey, Hey!

All night long.—— Hey, Hey!

Shoo rab - bit 'way. Hey, Hey! SHOO!

Rabbit Run

Rab-bit run on the fro-zen ground! *Who told you so?*

Rab-bit run on the froz-en ground! *How do you know?*

I caught a rab-bit, *uh-huh!*   I caught a rab-bit, *uh-huh!*

I caught a rab-bit, *Uh-huh!*   I caught a rab-bit, *oh!*

Tree'd a Rabbit

Verse 2

My dog tree'd a rabbit.
My dog tree'd a rabbit.
Gonna milk my cow, gonna catch
  her by the tail,
Gonna milk her in the coffee pot,
  pour it in the pail.
Now g'wan 'round/rabbit.
Now g'wan 'round/rabbit.

Verse 3

...Gonna catch that critter sittin' on
  that log. *(x2)*...

Verse 4

...My rabbit's gettin' my turnip top,
  (x2)...

Sea Lion

Chorus

Leader: Hey, hey, hey. Group: Sea Lion.

Won't you be mine? Sea Lion.

You don't do noth-in', Sea Lion.

But wax and shine. Sea Lion.

Verse 1

Way down yonder...
About the sun...
My mother called me...
A sugar plum...
(Chorus)

Verse 2

Old rabbit hip...
Old rabbit hop...
Old rabbit bit...
The carrot top...
(Chorus)

Verse 3

If I live...
To get twenty one...
I'm gonna marry...
Somebody's son...
(Chorus)

Verse 4

See that man...
With the blue shirt on...
You'd better leave...
That man alone...
(Chorus)

Fur, Feathers & Fins

Who's Got a Fish Pole?

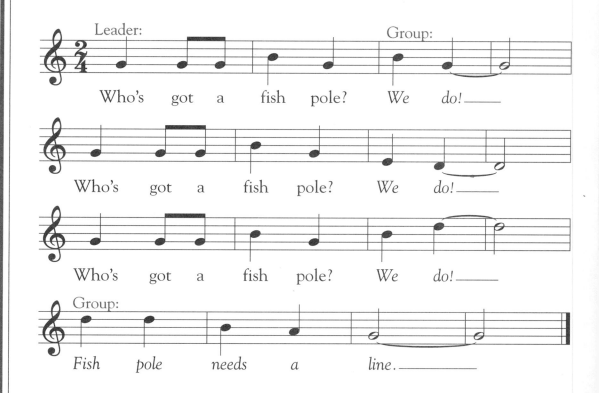

Leader:
Who's got a fish pole? Group: We do!

Who's got a fish pole? We do!

Who's got a fish pole? We do!

Group:
Fish pole needs a line.

Verse 2

Who's got a fish line?...
Fish line needs a hook.

Verse 3

Who's got a fish hook?...
Fish hook needs some bait.

Verse 4

Who's got a cricket?...
Cricket catch a fish.

Places Near & Far

Amasee

Take your part-ner down the line   A-ma-see*, A-ma-see.

Swing your part-ner   by the arm   A-ma-see,   A-ma-see.

Verse & Motions

*Amasee means "I must see."

The group forms two lines facing each other. The head couple sashays to the bottom of the set and swings each other by the arm and stays at the end. The two lines move one step toward the top. The new head couple sashays to the bottom of the set and swings each other with one arm. Continue until all have had a chance to be the head couple.

All Around the Kitchen

Call: Response:

All a - round the kitch-en, Cock-a - doo-dle, doo-dle, doo.

All a - round the kitch-en, Cock-a - doo-dle, doo-dle, doo.

Now stop right still, Cock-a - doo-dle, doo-dle, doo.

Put your hand on your hip, Cock-a - doo-dle, doo-dle, doo.

Let your right foot slip, Cock-a - doo-dle, doo-dle, doo.

Then do it like this, Cock-a - doo-dle, doo-dle, doo.

All a - round the kitch-en, Cock-a - doo-dle, doo-dle, doo.

All a - round the kitch-en, Cock-a - doo-dle, doo-dle, doo.

All stand in a circle with one child in the middle.

Motions

All around the kitchen
  Children walk in a circle.

Now stop right still
  The circle stops.

Put your hand on your hip
  All place right hand on hip.

Let your right foot slip
  All circle to the right walking step-close, step-close.

Then do it like this
  Child in the center demonstrates a repeated motion.

All around the kitchen
  All perform the motion while moving to the right.

As the song repeats children walk in a circle and a new child is chosen to be in the center.

Bonnie Highland Laddie

Solo:
Were you ev - er in Que - bec?

Group:
Bon - nie Lad-die, High - land Lad - die.

Solo:
Were you ev - er in Que - bec? My

Group:
Bon - nie High - land Lad - die.

Solo:
Way, hey and a - way we go!

Group:
Bon - nie Lad-die, High - land Lad - die.

Solo:

Way, hey. It's heel and toe, My

Group:

Bon - nie High - land Lad - die.

Chicka - Hanka

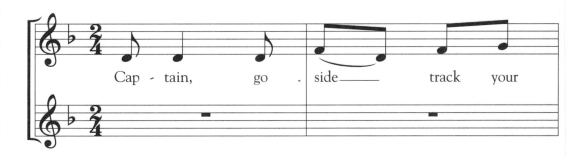

Cap - tain, go . side———— track your

train;————

chick - a - hank - a, chick - a - hank - a chick - a - hank - a, chick - a -

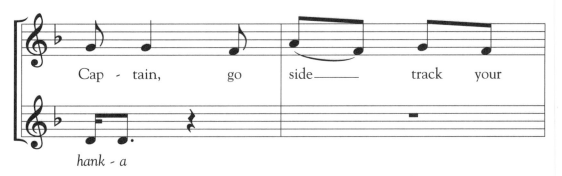

Cap - tain, go side———— track your

hank - a

train;————

chick - a - hank - a, chick - a - hank - a chick - a - hank - a, chick - a -

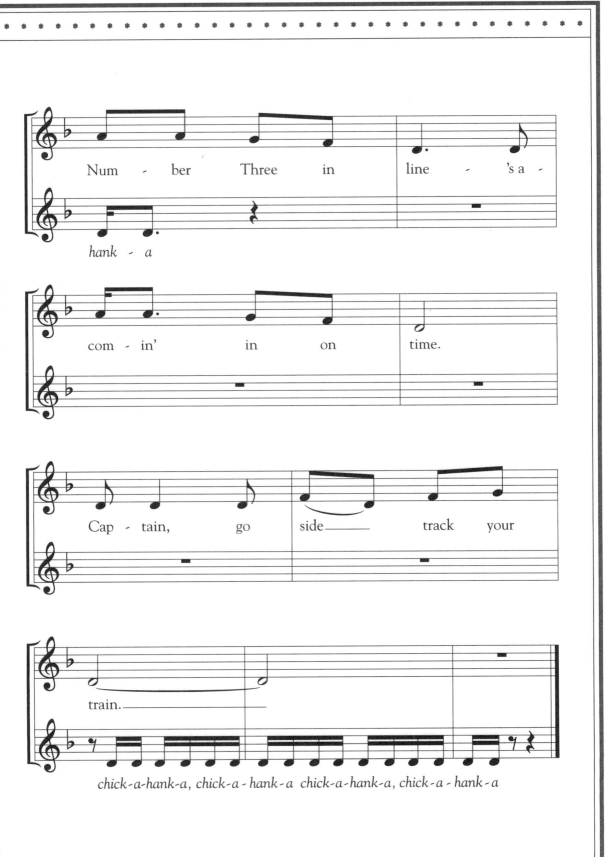

Did You Go to the Barny?

Leader: Did you go to the barn-y? Group: Yes ma'am.

Did you see my mul-ie? Yes ma'am.

Did you ride the mu-lie? Yes ma'am.

Group: And how did he ride? He rocked just like a cra-dle. He rocked just like a cra-dle.

Verse 2

Did you go to the barny? *Yes ma'am.*
Did you see my mulie? *Yes ma'am.*
Did you feed my mulie? *Yes ma'am.*
And what did you feed him? *I fed him corn and fodder, I fed him corn and fodder.*

Verse 3

Did you go to the milly? *Yes ma'am.*
Did you get any flour? *Yes ma'am.*
Did you bake any cake? *Yes ma'am.*
And why did you bake 'em? *I'll marry Sunday morning, I'll marry Sunday morning.*

Goin' Down to Cairo

1. Go - in' down to Cai - ro, *good - bye and a good - bye,*

2. Go - in' down to Cai - ro, *good - bye Li - za Jane.*

3. Black them boots and a-make them shine, *good - bye and a - bye - bye.*

4. Black them boots and a-make them shine, *good - bye Li - za Jane.*

Motions

Couples stand in a circle (girls to the right of the boys).

Phrases 1 & 2

Holding hands, all walk clockwise (16 steps).

Phrases 3 & 4

Grand right and left: All turn and face their partner. Hold partner's right hand, reach left hand to the person behind partner. Let go of partner and reach right hand to the person behind the person behind your partner. Continue alternating right and left hands until all arrive back to their original partner. Swing original partner around once and promenade counter-clockwise until the end of the verse.

(Repeat third and fourth phrases as many times as needed to complete the dance.)

Hashewie (Going Round) *Eritrea*

Leader:

Ha - shew - i - e,——— Shew - i -

Group:

e, Ha - shew - i - e,——— Shew - i -

e, Ha - shew - i - e,——— Shew - i -

e, Bi - ha - de ha - bir - na, Shew - i -

e, Ha - shew-i- e_e - na - bel - na, Shew - i -

e, A - lem kit - fel - to, Shew - i -

e, Ku - lu me - nin - et - na, Shew - i -

e, Ha - shew - i - e ni - bel, Shew - i -

e, Ne - fa - lit a - di - na, Shew - i -

e, Bi - ha - de ha - bir - na, Shew - i -

e, Ha - shew - i - e,____ Shew - i -

e, Ha shew - i - e,____ Shew - i -

e, Ha shew - i - e,____ Shew - i - e.

Motions

The group forms a circle. As they sing, the students walk to the right around the circle, stepping with the pulse of each downbeat.

General Translation

Going round and round, *round*
All together, *round*
Saying round, *round*
So the world would know, *round*
Who we are, *round*
Let's say, *round*
All together, *round*
Going round and round, *round*

Translation and Motions from *Roots and Branches* © 2009 Plank Road Publishing, Inc. Used with permission.

How Many Miles to Babylon

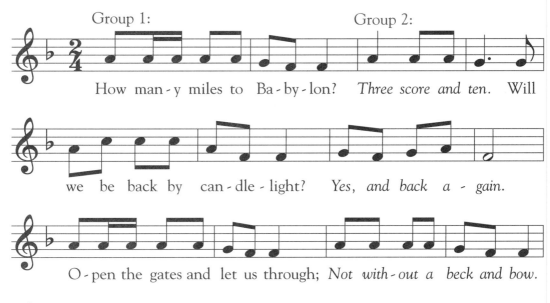

Group 1: How man-y miles to Ba-by-lon? *Three score and ten.* Will

we be back by can-dle-light? *Yes, and back a - gain.*

O-pen the gates and let us through; *Not with-out a beck and bow.*

Here's your beck, Here's your bow! *O-pen the gates and let us through.*

Motions

Two lines face each other. Both lines walk forward four steps and back four steps throughout the song. At the end of the song those in Line One hold hands and lift them up to form arches. Those in Line Two run through the arches as Line One advances forward. Both lines turn around to face each other again. The game is repeated as the lines switch roles.

I Got a Letter

Leader:

I got a let-ter this morn-ing,

Group:

Oh, yes!

I got a let-ter this morn-ing, Oh, yes!

Little Girl, Little Boy

Leader: Lit - tle girl, lit - tle boy. Group: Yes ma'am.

Well, did you go to town? Yes ma'am.

Well did you get an - y eggs? Yes ma'am.

Well did you bring them home? Yes ma'am.

Well did you cook an - y bread? Yes ma'am.

Well did you save me mine? Yes ma'am.

All: Then, shoo tur - key, shoo, shoo. Shoo tur - key, shoo, shoo.

Motions

Children stand in a circle during the call
and response. During the last phrase
children walk around in a circle "shooing"
the turkey with both hands alternating two
"shoos" on each side.

Shooliloo

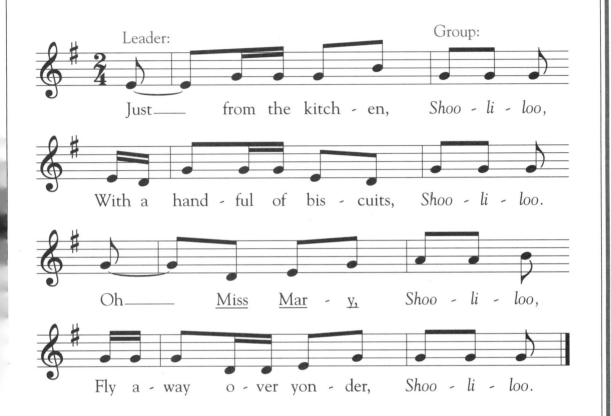

Leader: Just—— from the kitch - en, Group: Shoo - li - loo,

With a hand - ful of bis - cuits, Shoo - li - loo.

Oh—— Miss Mar - y, Shoo - li - loo,

Fly a - way o - ver yon - der, Shoo - li - loo.

Motions

Children sit in a circle on the floor with one space open. The leader substitutes a different child's name for "Mary." That child gets up and "flies" to the empty space in the circle.

Step Back, Baby

Leader:

Group:

Not last night but the night be-fore,   Step back ba-by, step back.

Twen-ty four rob-bers at my door,   Step back ba-by, step back.

O-pened up the door and let them in,— Step back ba-by, step back.

Hit 'um on the head with a   rol-lin' pin,   Step back ba-by, step back.

Stooping on the Window

Leader:
Stoop - ing on the win - dow,

Group:
Wind— the ball.

Stoop - ing on the win - dow, Wind— the ball.

Stoop - ing on the win - dow, Wind— the ball.

Stoop - ing on the win - dow, Wind— the ball.

Let's wind the ball, A - gain, a - gain, a - gain.

Un - wind the ball, a - gain, a - gain, a - gain.

Motions

Perform some hand clapping pattern with a partner throughout.

For Example:

Facing a partner perform the following with one motion per beat:

Clap own hands.

Clap right hand to partner's right hand.

Clap own hands.

Clap left hand to partner's left hand.

Clap own hands.

Clap both partner's hands.

Clap own hands.

Tap own legs with both hands.

Repeat entire sequence as often as necessary.

Places Near & Far

Way Down Yonder

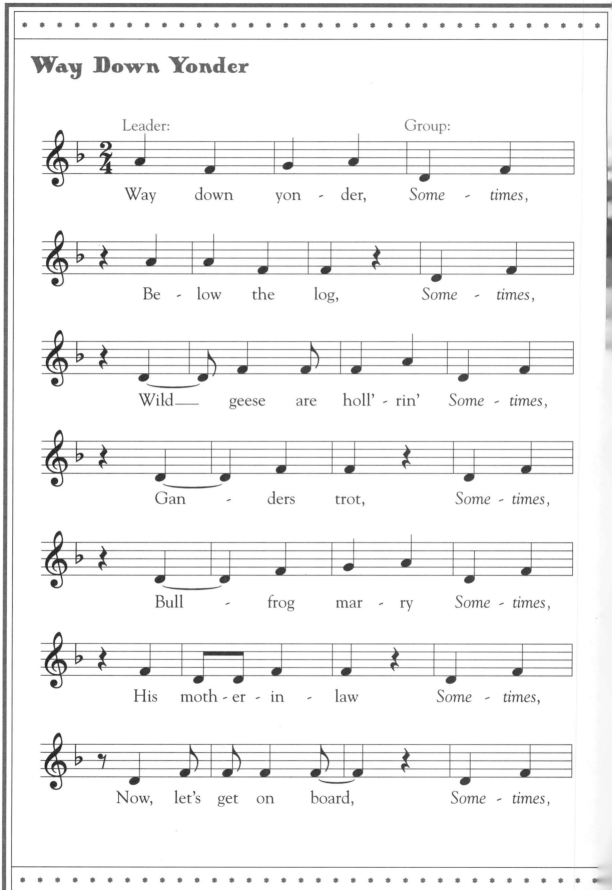

the book of call & respor

I'm goin' to ball that jack, Some - times,

Un - til my hon - ey comes back, Some - times,

I want to rear back, Jack Some - times,

And get a hump in my back, Some - times,

I'm goin' o - ver here, Some - times,

Goin' to get my pal, Some - times.____

Motions

Children stand in a circle while one child walks around the inside of the circle. Those in the circle alternate between clapping their own hands and reaching out to the sides in both directions to clap the hands of those on each side.

Way Down in North Car'lina

Leader:
Way down in North Car'-li-na (*whistle*) - - - - -

On the banks of Ole Tare Riv-er (*whistle*) - - - - - -

I go from there to Al-a-bam-a, (*whistle*) - - - - - -

For to see my ole Aunt Han-nah. (*whistle*) - - - - - -

Verse 2

Now Nancy, I must leave you...
Do not let our parting grieve you...
Dance and sing, forget your sorrow...
I'll be back sometime tomorrow...

Songs of Faith

Mary Had a Baby

Leader: Mar - y had a ba - by, Yes Lord!

Mar - y had a ba - by, Yes my Lord!

Mar - y had a ba - by, Yes Lord!

All: The peo - ple keep a com - in' but the train done gone.

Additional Verses

2. Where was He born?...
3. Born in a manger...
4. What you gonna call Him?...
5. Call Him King Jesus...

Dem Bones Gonna Rise Again

Leader:
D'Lord, He thought he'd make a man,

Group:
Dem bones gon - na rise a - gain. He

Leader:
took a lit - tle wa - ter and he took a lit - tle sand,

Group:
Dem bones gon - na rise a - gain.

Chorus
I know it, know it, in - deed I know it broth - er,

I know it Whee! Dem bones gon - na rise a - gain.

Motions for the Chorus

Tap legs on the beat and throw hands in the air on the word, "Whee."

Additional Verses

2. He took a rib from Adam's side...Made Miss Eve for to be his bride...
   (Chorus)

3. Put them in a garden fair...Thought they'd be so happy there...
   (Chorus)

4. Peaches, pears and plums and such...That apple tree you must not touch...
   (Chorus)

5. Old Miss Eve came walkin' 'round...Spied those apples on the ground...
   (Chorus)

6. 'Round that tree old Satan slunk...And at Miss Eve his eye he wonk...
   (Chorus)

7. She took a little peck and she took a little pull...Next thing she had an apron full...
   (Chorus)

8. Adam he came prowlin' 'round...Spied those peelin's all over the ground...
   (Chorus)

9. He took himself a little slice...Smacked his lips and said, "'Twas nice"...
   (Chorus)

10. Next day when the Lord came down...He spied those cores all over the ground...
    (Chorus)

11. "ADAM! Who these cores did leave?..." "'Twasn't me Lord, it must've been Eve..."
    (Chorus)

12. "Adam, y'all must leave this place...And earn your bread by sweat of your face..."
    (Chorus)

13. So, He gave them a hoe and He gave them a plow...And that's the reason we's workin' now...
    (Chorus)

Jubilee

Michael Row the Boat

Leader: Group:

Mich-ael, row the boat a-shore,   *Hal-le - lu - jah.*

Mich-ael, row the boat a-shore,   *Hal-le - lu - jah.*

Verse 2

Sister, help to trim the sail...
Sister, help to trim the sail...

Verse 3

Repeat verse 1.

Verse 4

Jordan River is deep and wide...
Milk and honey on the other side...

One Wide River

Leader: Group:

Old No-ah built him-self an ark, *one more riv-er to cross,*

He built it out of hick-o-ry bark, *one more riv-er to cross.*

All: (Refrain)

One wide riv-er,——— and that wide riv-er is Jor-dan.

One wide riv-er, there's one more riv-er to cross.———

Additional Verses

2. The animals came in two by two...
   The elephant and the
   kangaroo...(*Refrain*)

3. The animals came in three by three...
   The big baboon and the chim-
   panzee...(*Refrain*)

4. The animals came in four by four...
   Old Noah got mad and hollered for
   more...(*Refrain*)

5. The animals came in five by five...
   The bees came swarming from the
   hive...(*Refrain*)

6. The animals came in six by six...
   The lion laughed at the monkey's
   tricks...(*Refrain*)

7. When Noah found he had no
   sail...
   He just ran up his old coat
   tail...(*Refrain*)

8. Before the voyage did begin...
   Old Noah pulled the gangplank
   in...(*Refrain*)

9. They never knew where they were
   at...
   'Til the old ark bumped on
   Ararat...(*Refrain*)

Preacher Went A-Huntin'

Additional Verses

2. Carried along his shotgun...
3. Long came a grey goose...
4. Gun went a boo-loo...
5. Down came that grey goose...
6. He was six weeks fallin'...
7. Then they picked his feathers...
8. They were six weeks pickin'...
9. They put him on to parboil...
10. He was six weeks boiling...
11. They put him on the table...

12. The fork wouldn't stick him...
13. They put him in the hog pen...
14. Broke the hog's teeth out...
15. They took him to the sawmill...
16. The saw couldn't cut him...
17. The last time I saw him..
18. He was flyin' 'cross the ocean...
19. With a long strip of goslings...
20. They were all goin' "Quack, quack"...

Swing Low, Sweet Chariot

Chorus

Solo:

Swing low,   sweet char - i - ot,—

Group:

Com - in' for to car - ry me   home,

Solo:

Swing low   sweet char - i - ot,—

Group: *Fine*

Com - in' for to car - ry me   home.

Verse 1

Solo:

I   looked o - ver Jor - dan   and what did I   see,—

Group:

Com - in' for to car - ry me   home?

Solo:

A band of an - gels com - in' af - ter me,—

Group: *D.C. al Fine*

Com - in' for to car - ry me home.

(Chorus)

Verse 2

If you get there before I do...
Just tell my friends that I'm comin' too...
(Chorus)

Verse 3

I'm sometimes up and sometimes down...
But still my soul feels heavenly bound...
(Chorus)

Train Is A-Comin'

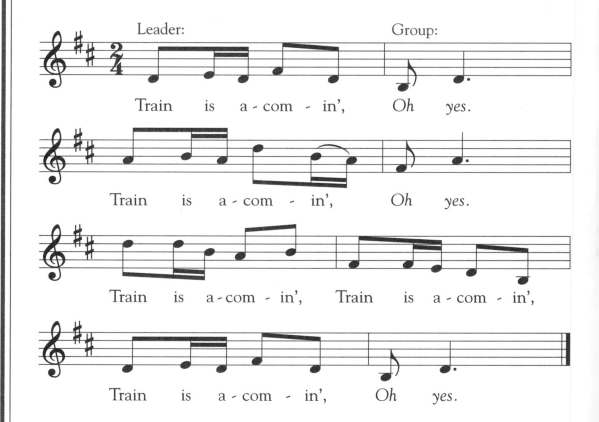

Verse 2

Better get your ticket...
Better get your ticket...
Better get your ticket, Better get your ticket.
Better get your ticket...

Verse 3

Room for many more...

Verse 4

Train is a-leavin'...

Wade in the Water

Chorus

Wade— in the wa - ter,— Wade— in the wa - ter, chil - dren. Wade— in the wa - ter,— God's a - gon - na trou - ble the wa - ter.—

Solo: See that band all dressed in white, Group: God's a - gon - na trou - ble the wa - ter. Solo: The lead - er looks like the Is - rael - ite, Group: God's a - gon - na trou - ble the wa - ter.—

(Chorus)

Verse 2

See that band all dressed in red...
It looks like the band that Moses
   led...
(Chorus)

Verse 3

Jordan's water is chilly and cold...
It chills the body but not the soul...
(Chorus)

Who Did Swallow Jonah?

Leader: Group:

Who did swal-low Jo-nah, *Who did swal-low Jo-nah,*

All:

Who did swal-low Jo-nah, down, down, down, down?

Verse 2

Whale did...Whale did...
(*All*) Whale did swallow Jo, Jo, Jo, Jo,
Whale did...Whale did...
(*All*) Whale did swallow Jo, Jo, Jo, Jo,
Whale did...Whale did...
(*All*) Whale did swallow Jo, Jo, Jo, Jo.
Whale did swallow Jonah...
(*All*) Whale did swallow Jonah down,
   down, down, down.

Verse 3

Daniel...Daniel...
(*All*) Daniel in the li, li, li, li.
Daniel...Daniel...
(*All*) Daniel in the li, li, li, li.

Daniel...Daniel...
(*All*) Daniel in the li, li, li, li.
Daniel in the lion's...
(*All*) Daniel in the lion's den, den,
   den, den.

Verse 4

Noah...Noah...
(*All*) Noah in the arky, arky.
Noah...Noah...
(*All*) Noah in the arky, arky.
Noah...Noah...
(*All*) Noah in the arky, arky.
Noah in the arky...
(*All*) Noah in the arky bailed, bailed,
   bailed, bailed.

Come Sail Away

Cape Cod Girls

Verse 1

Cape Cod girls they have no combs, *Heave a - way, heave a - way;*

They comb their hair with cod - fish bones, *We are bound for Aus - tra - lia!*

Chorus

Heave a - way my bul - ly, bul - ly boys, *Heave a - way, Heave a - way!*

Heave a - way and don't you make a noise, *We are bound for Aus - tra - lia!*

Verse 2

Cape Cod boys they have no sleds...
They slide downhill on codfish
  heads...
  (*Chorus*)

Verse 3

Cape Cod men they have no sails...
The sail their boats with codfish tails...
  (*Chorus*)

Verse 4

Cape Cod wives they have no pins...
They pin gowns with codfish fins...
  (*Chorus*)

Blow the Man Down

Solo:
Come, all you young sail - ors and lis - ten to me,

Group:
With your way, hey, blow the man down,

Solo:
Come all you young sail - ors and lis - ten to me,

Group:
And we'll give 'em some time for to blow the man down!

Additional Verses

2. Oh, blow the man down and we'll boot him around...

3. Now, I'll tell you a story all about the high seas...

4. Oh, it's not very short and it's not very long...

5. It's about a young sailor bound home from Hong Kong...

6. As I went a roving down Ratcliffe Highway...

7. A flash looking packet I chanced for to see...

8. She was bowling along her waind blowing free...

9. She clewed up her courses and waited for me...

10. She was round the counter and bluff in the bow...

11. Oh, where she did hail from I could not tell..

Haul the Bowline *16th-Century Sailing Song*

Solo:

Haul on the bow - line, the long tailed bow - line.

Chorus:

Haul—— the bow - line, the bow - line, Haul!

Verse 2

Haul on the bowline, the bully ship's
a rollin'.
(Chorus)

Verse 3

Haul on the bowline, Kitty you're my
darlin'.
(Chorus)

Verse 4

Haul on the bowline, the Old Man
he is growlin'.
(Chorus)

Pay Me My Money Down

Chorus (All sing)

Pay me, O pay me, Pay me my mon-ey down,

Fine

Pay me or go to jail, Pay me my mon-ey down.

Leader:

I thought I heard the cap-tain say,—

Group:

Pay me my mon-ey down,—

Leader:

To-mor-row is our sail-ing day.—

D.C. al Fine

Group:

Pay me my mon-ey down.

Verse 2

...The very next day we crossed the bar...
He hit me on the head with an iron
   spar...
(*Chorus*)

Verse 3

...I wish I was Mr. Jackson's son...
Sit on the fence and watch work
   done...
(*Chorus*)

Sing Hurrah, Boys

Leader: Group: Leader: Group:

Sing hur - rah, boys, *says he,* I'm the cook, *says he,*

First I leap, *says he,* then I look, *says he,*

On my ship, *says he,* I am king, *says he,*

If I cook it, *says he,* Then eat string, *says he.*

Verse 2

Give me water...
And some flour...
I'll bake bread...
In an hour...
Brown and firm...
Fresh and good...
You would swear...
It was wood...

Verse 3

Once a sailor...
Name of Dick...
Was as thin...
As a stick...

Then he ate...
Macaroons...
Now he's round...
As the moon...

Verse 4

My old captain's...
Tough and big...
And he eats...
Like a pig...
Took a great...
Bite of pork...
And he swallowed...
Up his fork...

Reuben Renzo

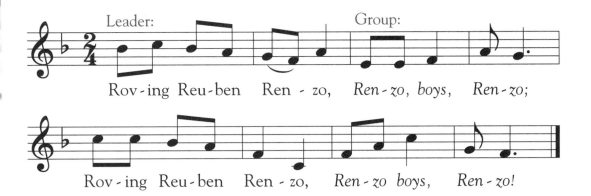

Rov-ing Reu-ben Ren - zo, Ren-zo, boys, Ren-zo;

Rov-ing Reu-ben Ren - zo, Ren-zo boys, Ren-zo!

Additional Verses

2. Renzo was no sailor...
   He might have been a tailor...
3. Renzo took a notion...
   That he would plow the ocean...
4. So he sold his plow and harrow...
   And likewise sold his barrow...
5. And Renzo had a pony...
   And sold him to a lady...
6. He went to London city...
   Where the ladies are so pretty...

7. He joined a lime juice whaler...
   And tried to be a sailor...
8. The mate he was a bad man...
   He took him to the gangway...
9. He gave him five and twenty...
   And that was plenty...
10. But the skipper, he was a fine old man...
    He took him to his cabin...
11. And taught him navigation...
    And now he plows the ocean...

So Handy

Solo:
Hand - y high and hand - y low,

Group:
Hand - y, me boys, so hand - y.

Solo:
Oh, it's hand - y high and a - way we'll go,

Group:
Hand - y, me boys, so hand - y!

Additional Verses

2. You've got your advance and to sea you must go...
   Around Cape Horn through frost and snow...

3. Growl you may, but go you must...
   Just growl too much and your head they'll bust...

4. Now, up aloft from down below...
   Up aloft that yard must go...

5. Now, one more pull and we'll show her clew!...
   Oh, we're the boys that'll put her through...

6. With a bully ship and a bully crew...
   And a bully Old Man to drive her through...

7. We're bound away around Cape Horn...
   And we'll get there as sure as you're born...

8. Now, one more pull and that will do...
   Oh, we're the gang that'll shove her through...

9. Now, here we are at sea again...
   Two months advance we're up against...

10. We're the gang that can do it again...
    Oh, we're the boys that'll do it once more...

A Yankee Ship

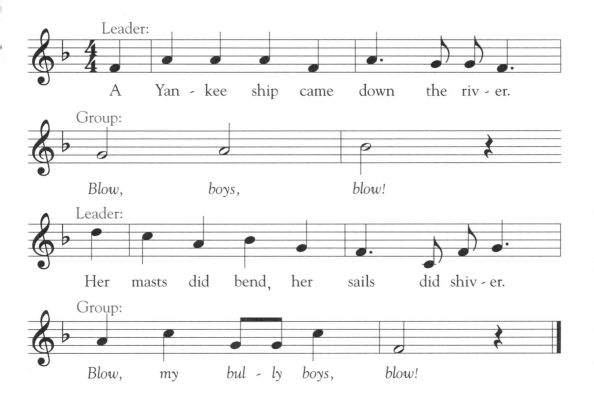

Leader: A Yan-kee ship came down the riv-er.

Group: Blow, boys, blow!

Leader: Her masts did bend, her sails did shiv-er.

Group: Blow, my bul-ly boys, blow!

Verse 2

And who d'you think was captain of her?...
Why, Bully Hayes was captain of her...

Verse 3

What do you think they had for dinner...
'Twas pickled eels' feet and bullock liver...

Verse 4

She sailed away for London city...
She never got there, more's the pity...

Index